THE MINDFUL DIGITAL NOMAD

BALANCING WORK, TRAVEL, AND WELL-BEING

CONNECTNOMADS

contact@connectnomads.com

THE MINDFUL DIGITAL NOMAD

Embark on a transformative journey with "The Mindful Digital Nomad: Balancing Work, Travel, and Well-being." This insightful guide delves into the challenges and rewards of a nomadic lifestyle, emphasizing the importance of mental and physical health. Discover practical strategies for maintaining balance, cultivating mindfulness, and prioritizing self-care while navigating the complexities of remote work and travel. From work-life balance and emotional resilience to mindful exploration and financial well-being, this comprehensive handbook offers indispensable tools to thrive in your nomadic journey, enabling you to forge a fulfilling and sustainable life on the road.

CONNECT NOMADS DIGITAL ELIBRARY

What is ConnectNomads.com

ConnectNomads.com is a comprehensive platform designed for digital nomads and remote workers seeking resources, guidance, and community. Offering valuable information on topics such as remote work opportunities, travel planning, and lifestyle management, ConnectNomads.com aims to empower location-independent professionals to thrive in their careers while exploring the world.

How this book is structured

This book is designed to serve as a comprehensive guide for digital nomads, offering insights and advice on various aspects of digital nomadism. It is not intended to be read in one go, but rather as a set of guidelines that provide valuable takeaways for different ideas and aspects of the nomadic lifestyle. As you explore the chapters, you may notice some overlap between topics, as certain strategies are commonly applicable across different areas. Feel free to read at your own pace, revisiting sections as needed, and drawing inspiration from the diverse range of concepts and techniques presented throughout the book.

If you have any ideas on new input, or even corrections, we are more than happy to hear from you, and if our editors like and accept the input then – if you are comfortable with it – we will include in our next update with credit noted for you.

Email us – contact@connectnomads.com

Mentions

We would like to clarify that throughout this book, we have not received any monetary gain or inducements for mentioning any connections, people, or resources. Our primary goal is to share valuable insights and tips that can genuinely help digital nomads in their journey of self-discovery and personal growth. The only exceptions to this are individuals or resources identified as ConnectNomads Members on our website. These members are part of our community and support our mission. We maintain transparency and prioritize the authenticity of the information shared, ensuring that our readers can trust the guidance provided in this book.

Our Digital Library

The ConnectNomads.com library offers members a diverse collection of free eBooks, providing invaluable insights and practical advice on a variety of topics related to the digital nomad lifestyle. From remote work strategies to travel tips and personal development, these eBooks are a valuable resource for location-independent professionals seeking to enhance their skills, knowledge, and overall experience.

Please visit http://www.connectnomad.com to see if there are any other publications which might interest you.

CONTENTS

INTRODUCTION

The Rise of Digital Nomadism

In recent years, the concept of location independence has gained significant traction, revolutionizing the way people live, work, and travel. Digital nomadism has emerged as a popular lifestyle choice for those who seek freedom, flexibility, and the opportunity to explore the world while maintaining a fulfilling career. Enabled by advances in technology and the growing acceptance of remote work, this movement continues to reshape traditional notions of work-life balance.

Digital nomadism is not just about working from a laptop on a beach or sipping coffee in a trendy co-working space; it's about embracing a mindset that values experiences and personal growth over material possessions and conventional definitions of success. It's about redefining what it means to live a meaningful life and seizing opportunities to learn, grow, and make a positive impact on the world.

As more people become aware of the potential benefits of a location-independent lifestyle, the demand for resources and guidance on how to successfully navigate this unconventional path has increased. "Digital Nomad Mastery: A Comprehensive Guide to Building a Successful Location-Independent Lifestyle" aims to provide aspiring and experienced digital nomads with the tools, knowledge, and inspiration they need to thrive in this exciting and ever-evolving landscape.

In this book, we will cover a wide range of topics crucial to achieving digital nomad mastery, from assessing your skills and finding remote work opportunities to managing finances, planning your travels, and adapting to new cultures. We will also discuss the importance of maintaining a healthy work-life balance, giving back to the communities you visit, and cultivating resilience and adaptability in the face of challenges.

By the end of this guide, you will have a solid understanding of the essential components of a successful location-independent lifestyle and be well-equipped to embark on your own journey toward digital nomad mastery. So, let's begin this adventure and explore the possibilities that await in the world of location independence.

The importance of mindfulness in a nomadic life

A location-independent lifestyle is a way of living and working that allows individuals to earn a living and pursue their passions without being tied to a specific geographic location. Enabled by advances in technology and the growing acceptance of remote work, this lifestyle offers the freedom and flexibility to design one's life around personal values, interests, and goals, rather than being constrained by conventional norms and expectations.

There are several different ways to achieve location independence, depending on one's personal preferences, skills, and circumstances. Some common approaches include:

1. Remote work: Many professionals are now able to work remotely for their employers, thanks to advancements in communication and collaboration technologies. Remote work allows employees to perform their tasks from any location, eliminating the need to commute or relocate for a job.

2. Freelancing: By offering their services as independent contractors, freelancers can choose their clients and projects, set their own rates, and work from anywhere. This can include professions such as writing, graphic design, programming, consulting, and more.

3. Running an online business: E-commerce, digital marketing, and other online ventures can be managed from virtually anywhere, making them a popular choice for location-independent entrepreneurs.

4. Passive income streams: Some digital nomads create passive income sources, such as investing in stocks or real estate, writing books, or creating online courses, which generate revenue without constant oversight, allowing them to travel and work on their own terms.

The location-independent lifestyle is not without its challenges, but the rewards can be significant for those who are willing to adapt and embrace the unconventional. "Digital Nomad Mastery: A Comprehensive Guide to Building a Successful Location-Independent Lifestyle" aims to provide aspiring and experienced digital nomads with the tools, knowledge, and inspiration they need to thrive in this exciting and ever-evolving landscape. By covering a wide range of topics, from assessing your skills and finding remote work opportunities to managing finances, planning your travels, and adapting to new cultures, this guide will help you navigate the complexities of living and working on your own terms, wherever your journey may take you.

ASSESSING YOUR SKILLS AND INTERESTS

Identifying Your Strengths

Before embarking on your journey towards digital nomad mastery, it's essential to take stock of your skills, strengths, and interests. This self-assessment will help you determine the type of remote work that aligns with your abilities and passions, setting you up for success in your location-independent lifestyle.

1. Reflect on your professional experience: Consider your past and current work experience. What roles, tasks, and responsibilities have you enjoyed and excelled at? This reflection can provide insight into your skills and areas of expertise that could be applied in a remote work setting.

2. Analyse your soft skills: Soft skills, such as communication, problem-solving, and time management, are crucial for remote work success. Think about your strengths in these areas and how they can contribute to your effectiveness as a digital nomad.

3. Identify your passions and interests: What are you truly passionate about, and how can you incorporate these interests into your location-independent career? For example, if you love writing and traveling, you might consider becoming a travel blogger or freelance writer for travel publications.

4. Take a skills assessment: There are various online tools and quizzes available that can help you identify your core strengths and areas for improvement. Taking a skills assessment can provide valuable insights into your unique abilities and potential career paths.

5. Seek feedback from others: Ask colleagues, friends, and family for their perspective on your strengths and areas of expertise. They may notice skills and abilities that you may not have considered, providing valuable input for your self-assessment.

6. Research in-demand skills and industries: Stay informed about trends in remote work and the digital economy. Identify which skills and industries are in high demand and consider whether you can develop expertise in these areas to increase your chances of finding remote work opportunities.

Once you have a clear understanding of your strengths, skills, and interests, you can begin to explore remote work opportunities and industries that align with your abilities and passions. This alignment will not only increase your chances of success but also contribute to a more fulfilling and sustainable location-independent lifestyle.

Choosing a niche or industry

After identifying your strengths, skills, and interests, the next step is to choose a niche or industry that aligns with your abilities and passions. This focus will help you stand out in the competitive remote work market and create a sustainable location-independent career. Here are some tips to help you choose the right niche or industry:

1. Evaluate market demand: Research industries and niches that have a high demand for remote workers or freelancers. Some sectors, such as technology, digital marketing, and content creation, have a higher demand for location-independent professionals. Focusing on these areas can improve your chances of finding remote work opportunities.
2. Assess competition: Analyse the competition within your chosen niche or industry. Is it saturated, or is there room for you to carve out a unique space for yourself? A less competitive niche can make it easier to establish yourself as an expert and attract clients or job offers.
3. Identify your unique selling proposition (USP): Determine what sets you apart from other professionals in your chosen niche or industry. Your USP could be a specific skill set, experience in a particular sector, or a unique approach to problem-solving. Emphasizing your USP can help you stand out and attract clients or employers.
4. Consider the potential for growth and development: Choose a niche or industry that allows for professional growth and development. As the remote work landscape evolves, it's essential to keep learning and expanding your skillset to stay competitive and relevant.
5. Align with your values and interests: Ensure that your chosen niche or industry aligns with your personal values and interests. A career that aligns with your passions is more likely to be fulfilling and sustainable in the long run.
6. Test the waters: Before committing to a particular niche or industry, consider taking on a few freelance projects or part-time remote work to gain experience and test your suitability. This hands-on approach will give you valuable insights into the day-to-day realities of working within that field and help you make an informed decision.

By carefully considering these factors and choosing a niche or industry that aligns with your strengths, skills, and interests, you will be well-positioned to build a successful location-independent career. The right focus will not only improve your chances of finding remote work opportunities but also contribute to a more fulfilling and sustainable digital nomad lifestyle.

Upskilling and professional development

To succeed as a digital nomad and stay competitive in the remote work landscape, continuous learning, upskilling, and professional development are crucial. As industries and technologies evolve, investing in your skills will ensure that you remain in demand and can adapt to new challenges and opportunities. Here are some strategies for upskilling and professional development:

1. Online courses and certifications: Many platforms, such as Coursera, Udemy, and LinkedIn Learning, offer a wide range of online courses and certifications in various fields. These courses can help you acquire new skills or deepen your existing expertise, making you more marketable to potential clients or employers.
2. Workshops and webinars: Attending industry-specific workshops or webinars can provide you with valuable insights and up-to-date information on trends and best practices. These events often offer networking opportunities, allowing you to connect with other professionals and learn from their experiences.
3. Conferences and industry events: In-person or virtual conferences and industry events can be an excellent way to stay informed about the latest developments in your field, learn from experts, and network with other professionals.

4. Networking and mentorship: Building relationships with experienced professionals in your niche or industry can provide valuable guidance, advice, and support as you develop your skills and advance your career. Seek out mentorship opportunities and engage with online communities, such as forums or social media groups, related to your field.

5. Reading and research: Stay informed about your industry by regularly reading relevant books, articles, and blogs. This habit will help you keep up with new developments and gain a deeper understanding of the trends and challenges in your field.

6. Hands-on experience: Seek opportunities to gain practical experience by working on real-world projects, whether through freelancing, internships, or volunteering. This hands-on approach will not only help you develop your skills but also build your portfolio and credibility in your niche or industry.

7. Personal projects and passion pursuits: Engaging in personal projects or passion pursuits related to your field can help you learn new skills, explore your interests, and demonstrate your abilities to potential clients or employers.

8. Soft skills development: Don't overlook the importance of soft skills, such as communication, collaboration, and time management. These skills are essential for remote work success and can be developed through practice, self-reflection, and seeking feedback from others.

By prioritizing upskilling and professional development, you will be better equipped to adapt to the changing remote work landscape and maintain a successful location-independent career. Investing in your skills and knowledge not only enhances your marketability but also contributes to personal growth and a more fulfilling digital nomad lifestyle.

FINDING REMOTE WORK OPPORTUNITIES

Freelancing vs. remote employment

When embarking on a location-independent lifestyle, one of the critical decisions you'll need to make is whether to pursue freelancing or remote employment. Both options offer unique advantages and challenges, and understanding the differences between them can help you determine the best path for your digital nomad journey.

1. Flexibility and control: Freelancing offers greater flexibility in terms of work hours, project selection, and the freedom to choose your clients. Remote employment, on the other hand, generally involves a more structured schedule and predefined job responsibilities.

2. Stability and benefits: Remote employees typically enjoy a stable income, benefits such as health insurance and retirement plans, and potentially more job security. Freelancers, however, must manage their own finances, find their clients, and handle the fluctuations in income that can come with project-based work.

3. Networking and collaboration: Remote employees often have the opportunity to collaborate with colleagues and develop relationships within their organizations, which can lead to professional growth and advancement. Freelancers need to actively network and build their professional connections to secure new projects and clients.

4. Skill development and growth: Freelancers have the advantage of diversifying their skillset by working on a variety of projects across different industries. Remote employees may have access to company-sponsored training and development programs, but their skill development may be more narrowly focused on their specific job role.

5. Accountability and support: Remote employees have the support of their organization, including access to resources, tools, and team members. Freelancers must be more self-reliant, managing their workload, client communication, and business operations independently.

6. Work-life balance: Both freelancing and remote employment offer the potential for improved work-life balance, but the specific nature of that balance can vary. Freelancers may have more control over their schedules, while remote employees might benefit from a more predictable work routine.

To choose the right path, consider your personal preferences, professional goals, and desired lifestyle. Evaluate factors such as your need for stability, the type of work environment you thrive in, and the level of control and flexibility you desire. By weighing the pros and cons of freelancing and remote employment, you can make an informed decision that sets you up for success in your location-independent journey.

Job boards and platforms for digital nomads

A critical step in establishing a successful location-independent lifestyle is finding the right remote work opportunities. Various job boards and platforms cater specifically to digital nomads and remote workers, making it easier to find jobs and freelance gigs that align with your skills and interests. Here are some popular options:

1. Remote.co: Remote.co is a curated job board featuring remote job opportunities in various industries, including IT, marketing, design, and more. The platform also offers valuable resources and insights for remote workers.

2. We Work Remotely: We Work Remotely is a popular job board that focuses exclusively on remote job opportunities. Job seekers can find opportunities in categories like programming, marketing, design, and customer support.

3. FlexJobs: FlexJobs is a subscription-based job board that offers a curated list of remote, freelance, and flexible job opportunities. The platform screens each job listing to ensure its legitimacy, providing job seekers with reliable options.

4. Upwork: Upwork is a widely-used freelance platform that connects freelancers with clients looking for various services, such as writing, graphic design, programming, and more. Users can create a profile, showcase their skills, and bid on projects that match their expertise.

5. Freelancer: Similar to Upwork, Freelancer is another platform that connects freelancers with clients seeking specific services. Freelancers can browse through available projects and submit proposals to clients.

6. Toptal: Toptal is a talent network that connects businesses with top freelance professionals, particularly in the fields of software development, design, and finance. The platform has a rigorous vetting process to ensure high-quality freelancers for their clients.

7. Remote OK: Remote OK is a job board that caters to digital nomads and remote workers, featuring opportunities in various industries, including tech, marketing, design, and customer support.

8. Working Nomads: Working Nomads is a curated job board offering remote job opportunities in a variety of fields. Users can browse through job listings and subscribe to email updates for new opportunities in their chosen categories.

9. LinkedIn: While not exclusively focused on remote work, LinkedIn is a valuable resource for job seekers. You can search for remote job opportunities using the platform's job search feature, and network with professionals in your industry to uncover hidden opportunities.

By exploring these job boards and platforms, digital nomads can find remote work opportunities that align with their skills, interests, and desired lifestyle. Regularly monitoring these resources and building a strong professional network will increase your chances of finding the perfect remote job or freelance project to support your location-independent journey.

Networking and building a professional online presence

Networking and establishing a robust online presence are essential for digital nomads, as they can open doors to new opportunities, collaborations, and valuable resources. Building a strong professional network and online presence will help you stand out in the competitive remote work market and increase your chances of success. Here are some strategies to help you get started:

1. Optimize your LinkedIn profile: LinkedIn is a powerful platform for professional networking and showcasing your expertise. Ensure that your profile is complete, up-to-date, and highlights your skills and achievements. Connect with professionals in your industry, join relevant groups, and actively engage with your network by sharing valuable content and insights.

2. Create a professional website or portfolio: Having a personal website or online portfolio is an effective way to showcase your work and demonstrate your skills to potential clients or

employers. Use your website to highlight your best projects, provide information about your background and experience, and share testimonials or recommendations from previous clients or colleagues.

3. Engage on social media: Use social media platforms like Twitter, Instagram, or Facebook to share your knowledge, engage with others in your industry, and showcase your personal brand. Follow relevant hashtags, join industry-specific groups, and participate in online discussions and events to expand your network and stay informed about trends and opportunities.

4. Attend virtual and in-person networking events: Conferences, webinars, workshops, and other professional events provide opportunities to connect with like-minded individuals, learn from experts, and build relationships that can lead to new opportunities. Look for events in your niche or industry and be proactive in introducing yourself to others.

5. Join online communities and forums: Participate in online communities and forums related to your field, such as Reddit or industry-specific forums. Engaging in these communities allows you to share your expertise, learn from others, and build your credibility as a knowledgeable professional.

6. Collaborate with others: Look for opportunities to collaborate on projects, guest blog posts, or podcast interviews with other professionals in your niche. Collaboration can help you expand your network, learn new skills, and increase your visibility in your industry.

7. Develop your personal brand: Cultivate a consistent and authentic personal brand across all your online platforms. This consistency will help you stand out and make a lasting impression on potential clients, employers, and connections.

8. Nurture your network: Networking is not a one-time activity. Keep in touch with your connections by sending periodic updates, sharing relevant articles or resources, and offering help when possible. Maintaining these relationships can lead to new opportunities and valuable referrals.

By investing time and effort in networking and building a strong professional online presence, you can create a solid foundation for your location-independent career. Developing meaningful connections and showcasing your expertise will help you stand out in the competitive remote work market and increase your chances of success in the digital nomad lifestyle.

SETTING UP YOUR LOCATION-INDEPENDENT BUSINESS

Business structure and legal considerations

Establishing a location-independent business requires careful planning and attention to legal and administrative details. Choosing the right business structure and understanding the legal considerations associated with operating a remote business are crucial for protecting your interests and ensuring long-term success. In this chapter, we will explore various aspects of setting up your location-independent business.

1. Business structure options: Choosing the right business structure will impact your legal liability, taxation, and administrative requirements. Common structures include sole proprietorship, partnership, limited liability company (LLC), and corporation. Each structure has its own advantages and drawbacks, so it's essential to research and consult with a legal or financial advisor to determine the best option for your specific situation.

2. Registering your business: Depending on your chosen business structure and jurisdiction, you may need to register your business with the appropriate government agency. This process typically involves choosing a business name, providing necessary documentation, and paying registration fees.

3. Legal and tax considerations: Operating a location-independent business can involve complex legal and tax issues, particularly if you're working across international borders. You'll need to consider aspects such as tax residency, double taxation agreements, and local regulations that may apply to your business activities. It's crucial to consult with a tax professional or legal advisor to ensure that you're complying with all applicable laws and regulations.

4. Business bank account: Opening a separate business bank account can help you keep your personal and business finances separate, making it easier to manage your financial records and prepare for tax filing.

5. International money transfers and currency conversion: As a location-independent business owner, you may need to deal with international money transfers and currency conversions. Research your options and choose a service or platform that offers low fees, favourable exchange rates, and convenient features.

6. Invoicing and payment processing: Implement a reliable invoicing and payment processing system to ensure that you're efficiently managing your cash flow and maintaining accurate financial records. Many tools and platforms can help you streamline this process, such as QuickBooks, FreshBooks, or PayPal.

7. Contracts and agreements: Establish clear contracts and agreements with your clients, outlining the scope of work, payment terms, and any other relevant details. This documentation will help protect your interests and prevent potential disputes.

8. Business insurance: Depending on your industry and specific business activities, you may need to consider obtaining business insurance to protect yourself from potential liabilities and financial risks.

By carefully considering the business structure, legal, and administrative aspects of setting up your location-independent business, you can lay a solid foundation for a successful and sustainable venture. It's crucial to research your options, consult with professionals, and stay informed about any changes in laws or regulations that may affect your business as you continue your digital nomad journey.

Branding and marketing your services

Creating a strong brand and effectively marketing your services are crucial components of building a successful location-independent business. Your brand is what sets you apart from competitors and helps potential clients understand the value you offer. In this chapter, we'll explore strategies for branding and marketing your services to attract clients and grow your business.

1. Define your unique selling proposition (USP): Your USP is the unique combination of skills, experience, and expertise that sets you apart from others in your industry. Clearly define your USP and communicate it through your marketing materials, website, and social media presence.

2. Develop a cohesive brand identity: Create a consistent brand identity that reflects your USP and resonates with your target audience. This includes your logo, colour scheme, typography, and tone of voice. Ensure that your brand identity is consistently applied across all your marketing channels.

3. Optimize your website: Your website should be user-friendly, visually appealing, and optimized for search engines to attract organic traffic. Include a clear description of your services, a portfolio of your work, testimonials from clients, and a compelling call-to-action to encourage potential clients to get in touch.

4. Content marketing: Share valuable, relevant, and engaging content through your blog, social media channels, or guest posts on other websites. Content marketing helps to establish your authority, build trust with your audience, and drive traffic to your website.

5. Utilize social media: Actively engage with your target audience on social media platforms like LinkedIn, Twitter, Instagram, or Facebook. Share informative content, join relevant groups, and participate in discussions to build relationships and demonstrate your expertise.

6. Email marketing: Build an email list of prospects and clients, and send regular updates, informative content, and promotional offers to keep your audience engaged and informed about your services.

7. Networking: Attend industry events, join online communities, and participate in forums to build relationships with other professionals and potential clients. Networking can lead to referrals, collaborations, and new business opportunities.

8. Client testimonials and case studies: Showcase positive client testimonials and case studies on your website and in your marketing materials to demonstrate the value you provide and build trust with potential clients.

9. Offer free consultations or resources: Provide free consultations, webinars, or downloadable resources to attract potential clients and demonstrate your expertise.

10. Monitor and adjust your marketing efforts: Regularly analyse the performance of your marketing efforts and adjust your strategies as needed. Track metrics such as website traffic, social media engagement, and conversion rates to understand what's working and where improvements can be made.

By developing a strong brand and implementing effective marketing strategies, you can attract clients and grow your location-independent business. Remember to stay consistent in your messaging, continually engage with your target audience, and adapt your marketing efforts as needed to achieve the best results.

Pricing, invoicing, and managing clients

Effectively pricing your services, managing invoicing, and maintaining positive client relationships are essential components of running a successful location-independent business. In this chapter, we'll explore strategies for setting prices, handling invoicing, and managing clients to ensure smooth operations and client satisfaction.

1. Pricing your services: When setting prices for your services, consider factors such as your experience, industry standards, the complexity of the project, and the value you provide to the client. Research competitor pricing and be prepared to justify your rates based on your unique selling proposition (USP). You may choose to price your services hourly, per project, or on a retainer basis, depending on your industry and preferences.

2. Creating professional invoices: Use a reliable invoicing tool or software to create professional invoices that include all necessary information, such as your business name and contact details, invoice date, payment terms, and a detailed breakdown of the services provided. Ensure that your invoices are consistent with your branding and provide clear instructions for payment.

3. Setting payment terms: Establish clear payment terms with your clients upfront, specifying when payment is due, accepted payment methods, and any late payment fees. Communicate your payment terms in your contract or agreement and include them on your invoices.

4. Following up on overdue payments: If a client's payment is overdue, follow up with a friendly reminder email or call. If the payment remains outstanding, consider implementing late payment fees or suspending work until payment is received.

5. Managing client expectations: Clearly communicate the scope of work, project timeline, and deliverables with your clients to ensure that expectations are aligned. Be transparent about any potential challenges or delays, and provide regular updates on the project's progress.

6. Communicating effectively: Maintain open and timely communication with your clients through your preferred channels, such as email, phone calls, or video conferences. Respond to client inquiries promptly and professionally, and be proactive in addressing any issues or concerns.

7. Asking for feedback: Request feedback from your clients throughout the project and upon completion to identify areas for improvement and ensure their satisfaction. Use client feedback to refine your services and enhance your client relationships.

8. Building long-term relationships: Aim to build long-term relationships with your clients by consistently delivering high-quality work, exceeding their expectations, and offering exceptional customer service. Cultivate repeat business and referrals by staying in touch with clients after project completion and offering ongoing support or additional services.

9. Managing difficult clients: If you encounter a difficult client, remain professional, and address their concerns calmly and objectively. If the relationship becomes untenable, consider whether it's in your best interest to continue working with the client or part ways amicably.

By implementing effective pricing, invoicing, and client management strategies, you can ensure smooth business operations and maintain satisfied clients. Consistently delivering high-quality work and excellent customer service will help you build a strong reputation, foster long-term client relationships, and grow your location-independent business.

MANAGING FINANCES AS A DIGITAL NOMAD

Budgeting for a nomadic lifestyle

Effectively managing your finances is crucial for a sustainable and successful digital nomad lifestyle. Budgeting for a location-independent lifestyle can be more complex than traditional budgeting, as it involves fluctuating income, varying living costs, and unexpected expenses. In this chapter, we'll explore strategies for creating and maintaining a budget that supports your nomadic lifestyle.

1. Track your income and expenses: Start by tracking your monthly income and expenses to gain a clear understanding of your financial situation. Categorize your expenses into fixed costs (such as insurance, subscriptions, and recurring bills) and variable costs (such as accommodations, transportation, and entertainment). Use a budgeting app, spreadsheet, or pen and paper to record your financial data.

2. Estimate your living costs: Research the living costs for your chosen destinations, considering factors such as housing, transportation, food, and activities. Websites like Numbeo and Expatistan can provide helpful cost-of-living information for various locations worldwide.

3. Create a monthly budget: Based on your income and estimated living costs, create a monthly budget that covers your essential expenses and allows for savings and discretionary spending. Allocate funds to categories such as accommodations, food, transportation, entertainment, and emergencies.

4. Build an emergency fund: Establish an emergency fund to cover unexpected expenses or financial setbacks, such as medical emergencies, lost or stolen belongings, or sudden changes in your income. Aim to save at least three to six months' worth of living expenses in a readily accessible account.

5. Save for long-term goals: Set aside a portion of your income for long-term goals, such as retirement, home ownership, or future investments. Consider using a high-yield savings account, investment account, or retirement fund to grow your savings over time.

6. Optimize your spending: Look for ways to reduce your expenses without sacrificing your quality of life. This could include choosing lower-cost accommodations, using public transportation, cooking your own meals, or taking advantage of free or low-cost entertainment options.

7. Manage currency conversion and international transactions: Be mindful of currency conversion rates and fees when managing your finances across multiple countries. Use a multi-currency bank account or a platform like Wise (formerly TransferWise) to minimize fees and ensure favourable exchange rates.

8. Monitor your financial progress: Regularly review your budget and financial progress to ensure you're staying on track with your goals. Adjust your spending habits and savings plan as needed to accommodate changes in your income, living costs, or priorities.

9. Maintain financial records: Keep accurate and organized records of your income, expenses, and tax-related documents for easy reference and tax preparation.

10. Consult with financial professionals: Seek advice from financial professionals, such as accountants or financial advisors, to ensure that you're making informed decisions about your financial planning and tax obligations.

By creating a realistic budget and actively managing your finances, you can enjoy the freedom and flexibility of the digital nomad lifestyle without compromising your financial security. Staying organized, disciplined, and focused on your financial goals will help ensure your long-term success as a location-independent professional.

Banking and international money transfers

As a digital nomad, navigating the complexities of banking and international money transfers is essential for managing your finances efficiently and minimizing fees. In this section, we'll discuss strategies for handling banking and international money transfers while living a location-independent lifestyle.

1. Choose the right bank account: Look for a bank account that offers features suited to a digital nomad lifestyle, such as no or low fees for international ATM withdrawals, online banking, and multi-currency support. Many online banks and fintech companies, such as N26, Revolut, or Monzo, cater to the needs of location-independent professionals.

2. Maintain a home-country bank account: It's often helpful to maintain a bank account in your home country for tax purposes, credit history, and receiving payments from clients. Ensure that your home-country bank offers online banking services and international wire transfers.

3. Open a local bank account if necessary: Depending on the duration of your stay in a particular country and your financial needs, it may be beneficial to open a local bank account. This can make it easier to pay for local expenses, manage currency conversions, and potentially reduce transaction fees.

4. Use multi-currency accounts: Multi-currency accounts, such as those offered by Wise (formerly TransferWise) or Revolut, allow you to hold and manage multiple currencies within a single account. This can help you minimize currency conversion fees and better manage your finances across different countries.

5. Understand currency conversion rates and fees: Be aware of the current exchange rates and any fees associated with currency conversions. Use a platform or service that offers competitive exchange rates and transparent pricing to minimize costs.

6. Leverage low-cost international money transfer services: Utilize low-cost international money transfer services like Wise, PayPal, or Payoneer to send and receive funds across borders. These platforms often offer better exchange rates and lower fees compared to traditional banks.

7. Schedule regular transfers strategically: If you need to make regular international money transfers, such as paying bills or sending money to your home-country account, schedule them strategically to take advantage of favourable exchange rates and minimize fees.

8. Monitor exchange rates: Keep an eye on exchange rate fluctuations and consider converting currencies when rates are favourable to maximize the value of your money.

9. Use credit cards with no foreign transaction fees: Choose a credit card that offers no foreign transaction fees, cashback, or travel rewards to minimize costs and make the most of your spending while abroad.

10. Protect your financial information: Be vigilant about protecting your financial information when using public Wi-Fi networks, ATMs, or online banking platforms. Use a virtual private network (VPN), ensure your devices are secure, and be cautious when providing personal information online.

By implementing these strategies for banking and international money transfers, you can efficiently manage your finances while living a location-independent lifestyle. Understanding your options and being proactive about minimizing fees and maximizing the value of your money will help you maintain financial stability and security as a digital nomad.

Taxes and insurance for digital nomads

As a digital nomad, it's crucial to understand and meet your tax obligations and ensure that you have appropriate insurance coverage to protect yourself and your business. In this chapter, we'll discuss strategies for handling taxes and insurance as a location-independent professional.

1. Determine your tax residency: Your tax obligations will depend on your tax residency status, which is typically determined by factors such as your physical presence in a country, your domicile, and your ties to a particular jurisdiction. Consult with a tax professional to understand your tax residency status and the associated tax obligations.

2. Understand your tax obligations: Research the tax requirements for both your country of residence and the countries in which you earn income. Be aware of any tax treaties or agreements between countries that may impact your tax obligations. Ensure that you're familiar with the tax filing deadlines and requirements for each relevant jurisdiction.

3. Maintain accurate financial records: Keep organized and accurate records of your income, expenses, and tax-related documents to simplify the tax preparation process and ensure compliance with tax laws.

4. Consult with a tax professional: Seek the advice of a tax professional with experience in international taxation and the digital nomad lifestyle. They can help you navigate complex tax laws, minimize your tax liability, and ensure that you're meeting your legal obligations.

5. Consider incorporating your business: Depending on your circumstances, incorporating your business in a specific jurisdiction may offer tax benefits or help simplify your tax obligations. Consult with a tax professional and legal advisor to determine whether incorporating your business is the right choice for your situation.

6. Health insurance: Obtain comprehensive health insurance that provides coverage for medical expenses, emergency evacuations, and repatriation in the countries you plan to visit. Many insurers offer plans specifically designed for digital nomads and long-term travellers, such as SafetyWing, World Nomads, or Cigna Global.

7. Travel insurance: In addition to health insurance, consider purchasing travel insurance that covers trip cancellations, delays, lost or stolen baggage, and other travel-related issues. Many travel insurance providers offer policies tailored to the needs of digital nomads and long-term travellers.

8. Professional liability insurance: If you're providing professional services as a digital nomad, consider obtaining professional liability insurance (also known as errors and omissions insurance). This type of insurance can protect you from financial losses due to claims of negligence, errors, or omissions in your professional services.

9. Equipment insurance: Ensure that your valuable equipment, such as laptops, cameras, and other electronic devices, is covered by insurance in case of loss, theft, or damage. Some travel insurance policies include coverage for personal belongings, or you may need to purchase separate equipment insurance.

10. Review and update your insurance policies: Regularly review your insurance policies to ensure that they continue to meet your needs and provide adequate coverage as your circumstances change. Update your policies as needed to reflect changes in your location, activities, or equipment.

By understanding your tax obligations and ensuring that you have appropriate insurance coverage, you can minimize financial risks and legal issues while enjoying the freedom and flexibility of the digital nomad lifestyle. Consulting with tax and insurance professionals can help you navigate complex regulations and make informed decisions about your financial protection.

PLANNING YOUR TRAVELS

Researching destinations and visa requirements

As a digital nomad, planning your travels is essential for a smooth and enjoyable experience. Part of this planning process involves researching potential destinations and understanding the visa requirements for each location. In this chapter, we'll discuss strategies for researching destinations and navigating visa requirements as a location-independent professional.

1. Determine your travel priorities: Before researching destinations, consider your priorities and preferences when choosing a location. Factors to consider include cost of living, climate, internet connectivity, safety, local culture, language barriers, and proximity to other destinations of interest.

2. Research potential destinations: Use resources like travel blogs, digital nomad forums, social media groups, and destination-specific websites to learn about the experiences of other digital nomads in various locations. These resources can provide valuable insights into the pros and cons of each destination, as well as practical tips and advice for living and working in each location.

3. Evaluate internet connectivity: Reliable internet connectivity is essential for most digital nomads. Research the availability, speed, and reliability of internet connections in your potential destinations. Consider factors such as Wi-Fi availability in accommodations, coworking spaces, and public areas, as well as the coverage and cost of mobile data plans.

4. Assess safety and security: Research the safety and security of each potential destination, considering factors such as crime rates, political stability, and natural disaster risks. Resources like the U.S. Department of State's Travel Advisories and the UK Foreign and Commonwealth Office's Travel Advice provide safety information and recommendations for travellers.

5. Understand visa requirements: Research the visa requirements for your nationality in each potential destination. Determine whether you need a tourist visa, business visa, or a specific digital nomad visa. Be aware of any restrictions on the duration of your stay, work permissions, and visa renewal or extension processes.

6. Consider visa-free travel options: Many countries offer visa-free travel or visa-on-arrival options for certain nationalities. Research these options to simplify your travel planning and minimize visa-related expenses.

7. Plan your travel itinerary: Once you've researched potential destinations and visa requirements, create a travel itinerary that takes into account factors such as seasonal weather patterns, regional events, and your personal preferences. Consider building in some flexibility to accommodate changes in your plans or to extend your stay in a particular location if desired.

8. Book accommodations and transportation: Research and book accommodations and transportation for your travels, taking into account your budget, preferred amenities, and proximity to coworking spaces or other resources. Consider using platforms like Airbnb, Booking.com, or specialized digital nomad housing websites to find suitable accommodations.

9. Prepare necessary documentation: Gather the necessary documentation for your visa applications, such as passport-sized photos, proof of sufficient funds, travel insurance, and any required invitation letters or supporting documents. Ensure that your passport is valid for the duration of your travels and has enough blank pages for visa stamps.

10. Stay informed about travel restrictions and updates: Keep yourself updated on any travel restrictions, entry requirements, or quarantine protocols related to COVID-19 or other health concerns. Monitor the news and official government websites for updates and be prepared to adjust your travel plans if necessary.

By thoroughly researching destinations and understanding visa requirements, you can plan your travels effectively and enjoy a smooth transition between locations as a digital nomad. Taking the time to plan ahead and gather the necessary information will help you make informed decisions and maximize your enjoyment of the location-independent lifestyle.

Booking flights and accommodation

Finding the best flights and accommodation is crucial for a successful digital nomad experience. In this section, we'll discuss strategies for booking flights and accommodations that suit your needs, preferences, and budget.

1. Use flight search engines and comparison websites: Utilize flight search engines like Google Flights, Skyscanner, or Kayak to compare prices and find the best deals on flights. Be flexible with your travel dates and consider alternative airports or layovers to save money on your flights.

2. Sign up for fare alerts: Subscribe to fare alerts from flight search engines or specific airlines to receive notifications of price drops or special offers. This can help you secure the best deals on flights as soon as they become available.

3. Join airline loyalty programs and frequent flyer schemes: Enrol in airline loyalty programs or frequent flyer schemes to earn points or miles on your flights. Redeem these points for future flights, upgrades, or other travel-related perks.

4. Leverage credit card rewards and travel hacking strategies: Use travel rewards credit cards to earn points or miles on your everyday spending, which can be redeemed for flights, accommodations, or other travel-related expenses. Research and implement travel hacking strategies to maximize your rewards and minimize your travel costs.

5. Research accommodation options: Explore various accommodation options, such as hotels, hostels, short-term rentals, or co-living spaces. Use platforms like Airbnb, Booking.com, or specialized digital nomad housing websites to find accommodations that suit your budget, preferences, and needs.

6. Read reviews and seek recommendations: Read reviews from other travellers or digital nomads to get a sense of the quality, amenities, and location of your potential accommodations. Seek recommendations from friends, colleagues, or online communities to find the best places to stay.

7. Consider long-term rental discounts: Many accommodation providers offer discounts for long-term stays, which can save you money if you plan to stay in one location for an extended period. Inquire about these discounts when booking your accommodations.

8. Book in advance, but not too far in advance: Booking flights and accommodations in advance can often secure better prices, but booking too far in advance can result in higher prices or limited availability. Aim to book your flights and accommodations 2-3 months before your planned travel date for the best balance of price and availability.

9. Utilize coworking and co-living spaces: Many cities around the world offer coworking and co-living spaces that cater specifically to digital nomads. These spaces provide a productive work environment, comfortable accommodations, and opportunities to connect with other location-independent professionals. Consider incorporating these options into your travel plans to enhance your digital nomad experience.

10. Confirm and reconfirm bookings: After booking your flights and accommodations, make sure to confirm your reservations and keep track of your booking details. Reconfirm your bookings a few days before your departure to ensure that everything is in order and avoid any last-minute surprises.

By implementing these strategies for booking flights and accommodations, you can ensure that your travel arrangements are tailored to your needs, preferences, and budget. Planning ahead and staying organized will help you enjoy a seamless and enjoyable digital nomad experience.

Packing essentials for a digital nomad

Packing efficiently is crucial for digital nomads, as it allows for more freedom and flexibility during travels. In this chapter, we'll discuss the essential items you should pack for a successful and comfortable location-independent lifestyle.

1. Lightweight and versatile clothing: Pack clothing that is lightweight, easy to layer, and suitable for various weather conditions. Opt for items that can be mixed and matched to create multiple outfits with minimal pieces. Consider choosing wrinkle-resistant and quick-drying fabrics for easy maintenance.

2. Electronics and chargers: Bring essential electronics such as your laptop, smartphone, and any necessary accessories like chargers, adapters, and cables. Consider investing in a universal travel adapter to ensure compatibility with different outlets around the world.

3. Reliable and secure backpack or luggage: Choose a high-quality backpack or luggage that is durable, comfortable to carry, and offers adequate security features such as lockable zippers or hidden compartments. Opt for a bag with a capacity of 40-50 litres to balance the need for space with the desire to travel light.

4. Travel documents and copies: Carry your passport, visas, driver's license, and other essential travel documents, as well as digital and physical copies of these documents in case of loss or theft. Store digital copies in a secure cloud storage service for easy access.

5. Travel and health insurance information: Bring your travel and health insurance policy information, including emergency contact numbers and policy numbers. Keep a copy of this information in your email or cloud storage for easy access in case of an emergency.

6. Toiletries and personal care items: Pack a compact toiletry bag with essential personal care items such as toothpaste, toothbrush, shampoo, conditioner, soap, razor, and any necessary medications. Opt for travel-sized containers to save space and adhere to airline liquid restrictions.

7. First-aid kit: Bring a small first-aid kit with essentials such as band-aids, pain relievers, antiseptic wipes, and any required prescription medications.

8. Travel security items: Consider packing travel security items such as a money belt, hidden pouch, or portable safe to secure your valuables and protect yourself from theft.

9. Portable power bank: Carry a portable power bank to charge your devices on the go, ensuring that you always have access to your essential electronics.

10. Travel accessories: Pack useful travel accessories such as a reusable water bottle, microfiber towel, collapsible laundry bag, and packing cubes to stay organized and comfortable during your travels.

11. Entertainment and leisure items: Bring a few entertainment and leisure items, such as a Kindle or e-reader, journal, headphones, or a lightweight hobby item like a sketchbook or deck of cards to unwind during your downtime.

By packing these essential items and focusing on traveling light, you'll be well-prepared for a comfortable and successful digital nomad experience. Remember to prioritize functionality, versatility, and durability in your packing choices to maximize efficiency and minimize the stress of living out of a suitcase or backpack.

STAYING CONNECTED AND PRODUCTIVE ON THE ROAD

Tools and technology for remote work

As a digital nomad, staying connected and maintaining productivity is crucial for success. In this chapter, we'll discuss the essential tools and technology you'll need to work efficiently and effectively while on the road.

1. Reliable internet connection: A stable and fast internet connection is vital for remote work. Invest in a portable Wi-Fi hotspot or a local SIM card with a generous data plan to ensure connectivity wherever you go. Research the availability and reliability of Wi-Fi in your accommodations and local coworking spaces.

2. VPN (Virtual Private Network): Using a VPN is important for securing your internet connection and protecting your privacy, especially when using public Wi-Fi networks. A VPN also allows you to access geo-restricted content and services from your home country.

3. Communication tools: Effective communication is essential for remote work. Utilize communication tools like Slack, Microsoft Teams, or Google Chat for team collaboration, and video conferencing tools like Zoom, Google Meet, or Skype for meetings and presentations.

4. Project management and organization tools: Stay organized and on top of your tasks with project management tools like Trello, Asana, or Notion. These platforms help you keep track of your tasks, deadlines, and progress, and can also be used for team collaboration.

5. File storage and sharing: Use cloud-based file storage and sharing services like Google Drive, Dropbox, or Microsoft OneDrive to access your files from anywhere and collaborate with team members in real-time.

6. Time management and productivity tools: Maximize your productivity with time management tools like Pomodoro timers, Focus@Will, or RescueTime. These tools can help you stay focused, manage your time effectively, and track your productivity.

7. Cybersecurity: Protect your devices and sensitive information with strong passwords, multi-factor authentication, and regular software updates. Consider using a password manager like LastPass or 1Password to securely store and manage your passwords.

8. Remote desktop access: If you need to access your home computer or office network while traveling, set up remote desktop access using tools like Chrome Remote Desktop, TeamViewer, or AnyDesk.

9. Travel-friendly hardware and accessories: Invest in lightweight and travel-friendly hardware, such as a compact laptop, noise-cancelling headphones, a portable keyboard, and a laptop stand or ergonomic mouse. These items can help you maintain a comfortable and efficient workspace on the road.

10. Backup solutions: Regularly back up your files and data using cloud-based storage services or external hard drives. This ensures that your work is protected in case of device loss, theft, or malfunction.

By leveraging these essential tools and technologies, you can stay connected, organized, and productive while living and working as a digital nomad. Adopting a proactive approach to maintaining your digital workspace will help you succeed in your location-independent lifestyle and enjoy the freedom and flexibility that it offers.

Time management and productivity hacks

As a digital nomad, managing your time effectively and maintaining productivity is crucial for success. In this chapter, we'll share some time management and productivity hacks to help you work efficiently and make the most of your location-independent lifestyle.

1. Establish a routine: Create a daily routine that incorporates work, breaks, exercise, and leisure time. Having a consistent schedule helps you stay on track, manage your time effectively, and maintain a healthy work-life balance.

2. Set clear goals and priorities: Start each day or week by setting clear goals and prioritizing your tasks. Focus on high-impact tasks that bring you closer to achieving your objectives and delegate or eliminate low-priority tasks that don't contribute to your goals.

3. Use the Pomodoro Technique: Break your work into focused intervals, typically 25 minutes long, followed by a short break. This technique, known as the Pomodoro Technique, can help you maintain focus, reduce burnout, and increase productivity.

4. Leverage time-blocking: Schedule dedicated blocks of time for specific tasks or activities, such as email, meetings, or deep work. Time-blocking helps you focus on one task at a time, reduces multitasking, and ensures that important tasks receive the attention they deserve.

5. Minimize distractions: Identify and minimize distractions in your work environment, such as social media, email notifications, or noise. Use tools like Freedom, Cold Turkey, or StayFocusd to block distracting websites or apps during your work hours.

6. Automate repetitive tasks: Streamline your workflow by automating repetitive tasks using tools like Zapier, IFTTT, or Automate.io. Automation can save time, reduce errors, and increase efficiency.

7. Embrace the "two-minute rule": If a task takes less than two minutes to complete, do it immediately. This simple rule, popularized by productivity expert David Allen, can help you tackle small tasks quickly and prevent them from piling up.

8. Set boundaries and communicate expectations: Communicate your work hours and availability to clients, colleagues, and friends to set clear boundaries and manage expectations. This helps to minimize interruptions and maintain a healthy work-life balance.

9. Track your time and productivity: Use time tracking tools like Toggl, Timeular, or RescueTime to monitor how you spend your time and identify areas for improvement. Analysing your time usage can help you optimize your schedule, eliminate time-wasting activities, and increase productivity.

10. Make time for self-care and relaxation: Ensure that you allocate time for self-care activities like exercise, meditation, or hobbies. Taking regular breaks and engaging in leisure activities can help reduce stress, prevent burnout, and maintain your overall well-being.

By implementing these time management and productivity hacks, you can work more efficiently, achieve your goals, and enjoy the freedom and flexibility of the digital nomad lifestyle. Remember to regularly assess and adjust your strategies to ensure that you continue to grow and succeed in your location-independent career.

Balancing work, travel, and leisure

Striking the right balance between work, travel, and leisure is essential for digital nomads to enjoy a fulfilling and sustainable location-independent lifestyle. In this chapter, we'll provide tips on how to find harmony between these aspects of your life while living and working on the road.

1. Establish a routine: Create a daily routine that includes dedicated time for work, leisure, and travel-related activities. A consistent schedule helps you maintain productivity, prioritize self-care, and ensure you're making the most of your time in each destination.

2. Set realistic expectations: Acknowledge that you can't see and do everything in a short amount of time. Prioritize experiences that are most important to you and accept that you may need to skip some activities to maintain a healthy work-life balance.

3. Slow travel: Embrace the concept of slow travel by staying in each destination for a longer period. This allows you to immerse yourself in the local culture, develop a deeper connection with the place, and maintain a more sustainable work schedule without feeling rushed.

4. Prioritize work during peak productivity hours: Determine when you're most productive and schedule your work hours accordingly. By focusing on work during your peak productivity hours, you can maximize efficiency and free up time for travel and leisure activities.

5. Set boundaries: Clearly communicate your work hours and availability to clients, colleagues, and friends. Establish boundaries that protect your work time and allow you to fully engage in leisure activities without feeling guilty.

6. Schedule downtime and self-care: Make time for regular breaks, exercise, meditation, or other self-care activities to maintain your physical and mental well-being. Incorporate these activities into your daily routine to ensure they remain a priority.

7. Plan and organize leisure activities: Research and plan your leisure activities in advance to make the most of your limited free time. This can help you avoid decision fatigue and ensure you're spending your leisure time on experiences that truly matter to you.

8. Learn to say no: Recognize that you can't participate in every social event, sightseeing tour, or networking opportunity. Be selective with your commitments and prioritize activities that align with your goals and values.

9. Embrace flexibility: While maintaining a routine is important, be prepared to adapt your schedule as needed. Unexpected events or opportunities may arise, so stay open to change and be willing to adjust your plans accordingly.

10. Reflect and adjust: Regularly assess your work-life balance and make adjustments as needed. Consider whether you're spending enough time on work, travel, and leisure, and identify areas where you can make improvements to achieve greater harmony.

By focusing on balancing work, travel, and leisure, you can create a sustainable and enjoyable digital nomad lifestyle that allows you to achieve your professional goals while exploring new destinations and experiencing personal growth. Remember that balance is an ongoing process, and it's essential to continually reassess and adjust your approach to ensure your location-independent journey remains fulfilling and successful.

ADAPTING TO NEW CULTURES

Language learning and communication strategies

As a digital nomad, adapting to new cultures and effectively communicating with locals is a crucial aspect of living and working abroad. In this chapter, we'll explore language learning and communication strategies to help you successfully navigate and integrate into different cultural environments.

1. Learn the basics of the local language: Before arriving at a new destination, familiarize yourself with essential phrases and greetings in the local language. Even a basic understanding of the language can help you navigate daily life and build rapport with locals.

2. Use language learning apps and resources: Leverage language learning apps like Duolingo, Babbel, or Rosetta Stone to build your language skills. Utilize resources such as iTalki, HelloTalk, or Tandem to connect with native speakers for language exchange and practice.

3. Practice with locals: Make an effort to practice your language skills with locals, whether through casual conversations, language meetups, or organized language classes. Engaging with native speakers can significantly improve your language proficiency and understanding of the culture.

4. Be patient and open-minded: Learning a new language and adapting to a new culture takes time and patience. Be open to making mistakes, learning from them, and embracing the learning process.

5. Observe and learn from the locals: Pay attention to the customs, social norms, and etiquette in your new environment. Observing and learning from locals can help you understand cultural nuances, avoid misunderstandings, and build positive relationships.

6. Use non-verbal communication: Body language, facial expressions, and gestures can be powerful communication tools, particularly when language barriers are present. Be mindful of your non-verbal cues and be receptive to those of others.

7. Leverage technology for communication: Use translation apps like Google Translate, Microsoft Translator, or DeepL to bridge language gaps when necessary. These tools can help you communicate more effectively and navigate unfamiliar situations.

8. Embrace cultural differences: Recognize and appreciate the diversity of cultures and customs you'll encounter as a digital nomad. Approach each new culture with curiosity, respect, and a willingness to learn and grow.

9. Maintain cultural sensitivity: Be aware of the cultural context and sensitivities in each destination, and adjust your behaviour and communication style accordingly. This awareness can help you avoid inadvertently offending locals or causing misunderstandings.

10. Build a support network: Connect with fellow digital nomads, expats, and locals to build a support network in each destination. These connections can provide valuable insights, advice, and assistance as you adapt to new cultures and environments.

By embracing these language learning and communication strategies, you'll be better equipped to adapt to new cultures, build meaningful connections, and make the most of your digital nomad experience. Remember that cultural adaptation is an ongoing process, and maintaining a positive, open-minded attitude is essential for success in your location-independent journey.

Understanding and respecting cultural differences

As a digital nomad, understanding and respecting cultural differences is essential for building positive relationships, avoiding misunderstandings, and enjoying a fulfilling location-independent lifestyle. In this chapter, we'll discuss strategies to help you develop cultural awareness and show respect for the diverse customs and traditions you'll encounter.

1. Research and prepare: Before arriving in a new destination, research the local customs, traditions, and social norms. Familiarize yourself with basic etiquette, religious practices, and cultural expectations to avoid inadvertently offending locals or violating cultural norms.

2. Observe and learn from locals: Once you've arrived, observe how locals interact, behave, and communicate in different situations. Learning from locals can provide invaluable insights into the nuances of the culture and help you navigate unfamiliar environments more effectively.

3. Practice active listening: When engaging with locals or fellow travellers from different cultural backgrounds, practice active listening. Show genuine interest in their perspectives, experiences, and cultural beliefs, and seek to understand their point of view before offering your own.

4. Be aware of cultural biases: Recognize that your own cultural background shapes your perceptions and beliefs. Be open to challenging your assumptions and embracing different ways of thinking, behaving, and communicating.

5. Show respect for local customs and traditions: Participate in local customs and traditions when appropriate and demonstrate respect for the cultural practices of your host country. This may involve dressing modestly, observing religious practices, or adhering to local etiquette during social interactions.

6. Be adaptable and flexible: Be prepared to adjust your behaviour and communication style to align with the cultural expectations of your host country. This flexibility can help you build stronger connections, avoid misunderstandings, and show respect for the local culture.

7. Be patient and open-minded: Accept that cultural differences can sometimes lead to confusion or miscommunication. Approach these situations with patience, curiosity, and a willingness to learn from the experience.

8. Learn the local language: Make an effort to learn at least the basics of the local language, as this can greatly enhance your understanding of the culture and improve your ability to connect with locals.

9. Seek diverse perspectives: Engage with people from different cultural backgrounds to broaden your understanding of the world and challenge your assumptions. This exposure can help you develop a more open-minded and empathetic approach to cultural differences.

10. Reflect on your experiences: Regularly reflect on your experiences and interactions with different cultures to assess your growth in cultural understanding and identify areas for improvement. This introspection can help you become a more culturally aware and sensitive traveller.

By actively working to understand and respect cultural differences, you'll not only enrich your digital nomad experience but also develop valuable skills in cross-cultural communication and empathy.

Embracing cultural diversity and demonstrating respect for the customs and traditions of your host countries will enable you to forge lasting connections and enjoy a more rewarding location-independent lifestyle.

Building relationships with locals

Forming genuine connections with locals is a rewarding aspect of the digital nomad lifestyle, providing opportunities for cultural exchange, personal growth, and deeper experiences in your host countries. In this chapter, we'll discuss strategies for building relationships with locals and integrating into local communities.

1. Learn the language: Making an effort to learn and speak the local language can significantly improve your ability to connect with locals. Even a basic understanding demonstrates respect for the culture and encourages locals to engage with you more openly.

2. Participate in local events and activities: Attend community gatherings, cultural events, festivals, or local meetups to engage with locals and experience their culture firsthand. This involvement provides opportunities for building connections and learning more about the community.

3. Volunteer or join local clubs: Look for volunteering opportunities or join clubs or organizations where you can contribute your skills, passions, or interests. This not only helps you meet locals but also demonstrates your commitment to giving back to the community.

4. Be open and approachable: Display a friendly and approachable demeanour, making yourself available for conversations and interactions with locals. A warm smile, open body language, and genuine interest in others can go a long way in initiating connections.

5. Show genuine interest and curiosity: When engaging with locals, ask open-ended questions about their lives, interests, and perspectives. Be genuinely curious and interested in their stories, as this fosters deeper connections and encourages more meaningful conversations.

6. Respect cultural differences: Be mindful of cultural norms and expectations, and adjust your behaviour accordingly. Demonstrating respect for local customs, traditions, and etiquette can help you build trust and rapport with locals.

7. Offer help and support: Be willing to lend a hand or offer assistance when appropriate. Small acts of kindness can create a positive impression and contribute to building lasting connections with locals.

8. Share your own culture. Be open to sharing your own culture, experiences, and perspectives, fostering a mutual exchange of ideas and understanding. This can help build deeper connections and strengthen your relationships with locals.

9. Maintain communication: Keep in touch with locals you've connected with, even after leaving their country. Cultivate these relationships through regular communication, expressing genuine interest in their lives and well-being.

10. Be patient and persistent: Building relationships with locals takes time and effort. Be patient, persistent, and open to new experiences, and you'll gradually forge meaningful connections that can enrich your digital nomad journey.

By actively engaging with local communities and investing in relationships with locals, you'll experience a more immersive and authentic side of each destination. Embracing this aspect of the digital nomad lifestyle can lead to personal growth, cultural understanding, and a more fulfilling and rewarding journey overall.

HEALTH AND WELL-BEING FOR DIGITAL NOMADS

Staying physically and mentally healthy

Maintaining good physical and mental health is essential for digital nomads to enjoy a sustainable and fulfilling location-independent lifestyle. In this chapter, we'll discuss strategies for staying healthy, both physically and mentally, while living and working on the road.

1. Establish a routine: Create a daily routine that includes dedicated time for work, exercise, self-care, and relaxation. Consistency in your schedule helps maintain overall health and well-being, while also ensuring you stay productive and make the most of your time in each destination.

2. Eat a balanced diet: Prioritize nutritious meals and maintain a balanced diet to ensure you have the energy and mental clarity needed for a demanding nomadic lifestyle. Discover local food options and adapt your diet to incorporate healthy choices.

3. Exercise regularly: Incorporate regular physical activity into your routine to maintain your fitness, reduce stress, and boost your mood. Explore various forms of exercise, such as yoga, running, swimming, or group fitness classes, to find what works best for you and your lifestyle.

4. Prioritize sleep: Ensure you get enough quality sleep to support your physical and mental health. Establish a consistent sleep schedule, create a comfortable sleep environment, and minimize exposure to screens and stimulants before bedtime.

5. Stay connected with loved ones: Maintain regular communication with friends and family back home to stay emotionally grounded and supported. Schedule regular video calls or send updates to share your experiences and stay connected.

6. Practice mindfulness and self-care: Incorporate mindfulness practices such as meditation, deep breathing, or journaling into your daily routine to manage stress and maintain mental well-being. Set aside time for self-care activities that bring you joy and relaxation.

7. Manage work-related stress: Establish boundaries between work and leisure, and set realistic expectations for your workload. Utilize time management and productivity techniques to minimize work-related stress and maintain a healthy work-life balance.

8. Seek professional help when needed: Don't hesitate to seek professional help if you're struggling with physical or mental health issues. Tolomedicine and online therapy platforms can provide accessible and convenient support, regardless of your location.

9. Stay up-to-date with vaccinations and medical check-ups: Regularly consult with your healthcare provider to ensure your vaccinations are up-to-date and schedule routine medical check-ups to monitor your overall health.

10. Build a support network: Connect with fellow digital nomads, expats, and locals to build a support network in each destination. These connections can offer valuable advice, encouragement, and camaraderie to help you maintain your well-being while living and working abroad.

By prioritizing your health and well-being as a digital nomad, you'll be better equipped to face the challenges and enjoy the rewards of a location-independent lifestyle. Remember that self-care is an ongoing process, and it's essential to continually reassess and adjust your approach to ensure you stay healthy, happy, and productive on your digital nomad journey.

Coping with loneliness and isolation

The digital nomad lifestyle can sometimes be accompanied by feelings of loneliness and isolation, especially when moving frequently between locations or living in unfamiliar environments. In this chapter, we'll discuss strategies for coping with loneliness and fostering a sense of community while living a location-independent lifestyle.

1. Establish a routine: Creating a consistent daily routine helps provide structure and familiarity, reducing feelings of loneliness and disconnection. Include social activities and regular interactions with others in your routine.

2. Engage with local communities: Attend local events, workshops, or meetups to connect with locals and fellow travellers. Engaging with local communities can provide a sense of belonging and help you forge meaningful connections.

3. Join online groups and forums: Connect with like-minded individuals through digital nomad forums, social media groups, or networking platforms like Meetup. These online communities can offer support, advice, and opportunities for virtual socializing.

4. Connect with fellow digital nomads: Seek out coworking spaces, cafes, or other venues where digital nomads gather to work and socialize. Building connections with others who share your lifestyle can help combat feelings of loneliness and provide a supportive network.

5. Maintain regular contact with loved ones: Schedule frequent video calls or send updates to friends and family back home. Staying connected with your support network can help alleviate feelings of isolation and maintain a sense of emotional stability.

6. Practice self-care and mindfulness: Prioritize self-care activities like exercise, relaxation, or hobbies that bring joy and fulfilment. Incorporate mindfulness practices such as meditation or journaling to help process emotions and cope with feelings of loneliness.

7. Consider long-term stays: If you find constant travel exacerbates feelings of loneliness, consider staying in one location for longer periods. This allows you to establish deeper connections with locals, develop a routine, and create a sense of belonging.

8. Pursue shared interests: Join clubs, classes, or groups that align with your interests or hobbies. Participating in activities with others who share your passions can help you form meaningful connections and reduce feelings of isolation.

9. Be open to making new friends: Be approachable and open to meeting new people, even if it's just for a short time. Casual friendships and brief connections can still provide valuable support and companionship on your journey.

10. Seek professional help if needed: If feelings of loneliness or isolation become overwhelming or persistent, consider seeking professional help from a therapist or counsellor. Online therapy platforms can provide accessible support regardless of your location.

By actively addressing feelings of loneliness and isolation, you can create a more fulfilling and enjoyable digital nomad experience. Building connections, fostering a sense of community, and prioritizing self-care are crucial to maintaining emotional well-being and ensuring a sustainable location-independent lifestyle.

Establishing routines and self-care practices

Developing routines and self-care practices is essential for digital nomads to maintain a healthy work-life balance, manage stress, and ensure overall well-being. In this chapter, we'll discuss strategies for establishing routines and incorporating self-care practices into your location-independent lifestyle.

1. Design a daily routine: Create a daily routine that includes time for work, exercise, meals, self-care, and relaxation. A consistent schedule helps maintain productivity, balance, and well-being, while also allowing you to make the most of your time in each destination.

2. Set boundaries for work and leisure: Establish clear boundaries between work and leisure to ensure you're not constantly "on" and can fully enjoy your downtime. Dedicate specific hours for work and disconnect from devices during non-work hours.

3. Prioritize physical activity: Incorporate regular exercise into your routine to support physical and mental health. Choose activities that you enjoy and can do consistently, regardless of your location, such as yoga, running, or bodyweight exercises.

4. Plan for nutritious meals: Allocate time in your routine for planning, shopping, and preparing healthy meals. Eating well helps to maintain energy levels, mental clarity, and overall health, which are essential for a sustainable digital nomad lifestyle.

5. Develop a sleep schedule: Prioritize sleep by establishing a consistent bedtime and wake-up time. Create a relaxing pre-sleep routine and optimize your sleep environment to ensure you get adequate rest.

6. Stay connected with loved ones: Schedule regular check-ins with friends and family to maintain emotional support and connection. Staying in touch with your support network can help alleviate feelings of loneliness and isolation.

7. Practice mindfulness and meditation: Incorporate mindfulness practices, such as meditation, deep breathing, or journaling, into your daily routine. These practices can help manage stress, improve focus, and maintain mental well-being.

8. Dedicate time for hobbies and interests: Allocate time in your routine for hobbies and interests that bring you joy and relaxation. Pursuing passions outside of work helps maintain a sense of balance and fulfilment.

9. Set aside time for reflection and self-assessment: Regularly evaluate your routine, goals, and self-care practices to ensure they continue to support your well-being and align with your priorities. Make adjustments as needed to maintain balance and satisfaction in your life.

10. Be flexible and adaptable: While routines provide structure and stability, it's essential to remain flexible and adaptable as your circumstances change. Allow yourself to modify your routine as needed, embracing new experiences and challenges as they arise.

By establishing routines and self-care practices, you can better manage the demands of a location-independent lifestyle while maintaining a sense of balance, health, and happiness. Continually assess and adjust your approach to ensure you stay productive, fulfilled, and healthy on your digital nomad journey.

GIVING BACK AND MAKING A POSITIVE IMPACT

Supporting local communities and economies

As a digital nomad, you have the unique opportunity to make a positive impact on the local communities and economies you visit. In this chapter, we'll discuss ways you can give back and contribute positively to the places you call home, even if it's just for a short while.

1. Shop and dine locally: Support local businesses by shopping at local markets, dining at locally-owned restaurants, and purchasing products made by local artisans. This helps to stimulate the local economy and contributes to the community's well-being.

2. Hire local services: Whenever possible, hire local service providers such as tour guides, translators, or drivers. This not only supports the local economy but also allows you to gain deeper insights into the local culture and customs.

3. Be a responsible tourist: Respect local customs, traditions, and the environment. Follow guidelines for responsible tourism, such as minimizing waste, conserving water and energy, and respecting local wildlife and habitats.

4. Volunteer your time and skills: Seek out opportunities to volunteer your skills or time to local organizations, schools, or community projects. This not only benefits the community but also allows you to forge deeper connections and gain a greater understanding of local issues.

5. Donate to local causes: Consider making financial contributions to local charities, non-profit organizations, or community projects. Research reputable organizations and support causes that resonate with you and align with the needs of the local community.

6. Share your knowledge and expertise: Offer workshops, training sessions, or mentorship to locals in your area of expertise. Sharing your skills and knowledge can have a lasting impact on individuals and communities, empowering them to develop their own abilities and opportunities.

7. Engage in cultural exchange: Foster mutual understanding and respect by participating in cultural exchanges with locals. Share your own culture and experiences while learning about and embracing the local way of life.

8. Advocate for sustainable practices: Promote and practice sustainable tourism and responsible digital nomadism. Encourage fellow travellers and digital nomads to adopt sustainable practices and support local communities.

9. Connect with local digital nomad communities: Collaborate with other digital nomads in the area to support local initiatives, share resources, and exchange ideas on how to make a positive impact as a collective.

10. Share your experiences and raise awareness: Use your platform, whether it's a blog, social media, or personal conversations, to raise awareness about the places you visit and the issues they face. Inspire others to support local communities and make responsible choices while traveling.

By actively engaging in positive impact activities and supporting local communities, you can contribute to the well-being of the places you visit and create a more meaningful and rewarding digital nomad experience. Embrace the opportunity to make a difference and create lasting connections with the people and places that become a part of your journey.

Volunteering and responsible travel

As a digital nomad, incorporating volunteering and responsible travel practices into your lifestyle can enhance your experience and create a positive impact on the communities you visit. In this chapter, we'll discuss strategies for engaging in volunteer work and embracing responsible travel principles.

1. Research volunteer opportunities: Investigate volunteer programs and opportunities that align with your interests, skills, and the needs of the local community. Look for reputable organizations that prioritize ethical and responsible practices.

2. Choose sustainable projects: Opt for volunteer programs that focus on long-term, sustainable solutions and empower local communities. Avoid projects that promote dependency or undermine local initiatives.

3. Be mindful of your skillset: Seek volunteer opportunities that match your skills and expertise. This ensures that you're able to provide valuable contributions and make a meaningful impact during your time volunteering.

4. Commit to adequate time: When possible, commit to spending a sufficient amount of time on a project to ensure continuity and effectiveness. Short-term volunteering can be helpful, but longer-term commitments can lead to more substantial results.

5. Practice cultural sensitivity: Be respectful and open-minded when engaging with local communities. Learn about local customs, traditions, and norms to ensure your volunteer efforts are culturally appropriate and sensitive.

6. Embrace responsible travel principles: Follow responsible travel guidelines, such as minimizing your environmental footprint, respecting local customs, and supporting local businesses. These practices help to preserve local cultures and environments while also benefiting the communities you visit.

7. Educate yourself about the community and its needs: Take the time to learn about the specific challenges and needs of the community you're volunteering in. This knowledge will help you better understand how your efforts can contribute to the community's well-being.

8. Reflect on your motivations and expectations: Consider your reasons for volunteering and set realistic expectations about the impact you can make. Reflect on your experience and the lessons you've learned to inform your future volunteer work and travel decisions.

9. Share your experiences: Use your platform, such as a blog or social media, to raise awareness about the volunteer projects you participate in and the communities you visit. Inspire others to engage in responsible travel and volunteer work.

10. Continue your support: After your volunteer work is completed, stay involved by following the progress of the project, maintaining relationships with the community, and providing ongoing support when needed.

By combining volunteering with responsible travel practices, digital nomads can make a meaningful impact on the communities they visit while also enriching their own experiences. Embrace the opportunity to learn from and contribute to the communities you encounter, and create lasting connections that extend beyond your time spent volunteering.

Fostering a sustainable digital nomad lifestyle

A sustainable digital nomad lifestyle prioritizes long-term well-being, minimizes negative environmental and social impacts, and actively contributes to the betterment of the communities visited. In this chapter, we'll discuss strategies for fostering a sustainable digital nomad lifestyle.

1. Minimize your environmental footprint: Adopt eco-friendly practices such as reducing waste, conserving energy and water, using public transportation, and selecting accommodations with sustainable initiatives. These actions contribute to preserving the environment for future generations.

2. Support local economies: Prioritize spending at locally-owned businesses, hiring local services, and purchasing local products. By doing so, you help support local entrepreneurs and contribute to the community's economic well-being.

3. Practice responsible tourism: Respect local customs, traditions, and the environment. Follow guidelines for responsible tourism, and be mindful of your impact on local cultures and natural resources.

4. Engage in volunteer work: Contribute your time and skills to local projects or organizations that align with your interests and expertise. Volunteering can create a positive impact on the communities you visit and enhance your own experience.

5. Foster cultural exchange: Build connections with locals and fellow travellers, and participate in cultural exchanges that promote mutual understanding, respect, and appreciation.

6. Prioritize self-care and well-being: Establish routines and self-care practices that support your physical, emotional, and mental well-being. A sustainable lifestyle requires maintaining a healthy balance between work, travel, and personal needs.

7. Embrace slow travel: Opt for longer stays in destinations, allowing you to immerse yourself in the local culture, reduce your environmental impact, and foster deeper connections with the community.

8. Invest in eco-friendly gear and technology: Choose travel and work equipment that is environmentally friendly, durable, and energy-efficient. This helps reduce waste and the overall environmental impact of your lifestyle.

9. Advocate for sustainable practices: Share your sustainable practices with fellow digital nomads and travellers, and encourage others to adopt environmentally and socially responsible behaviours.

10. Continuously learn and adapt: Stay informed about sustainable living practices, and be open to adjusting your lifestyle as new information becomes available. Embrace lifelong learning as a key component of a sustainable digital nomad lifestyle.

By fostering a sustainable digital nomad lifestyle, you can minimize your negative impact on the environment and communities, while maximizing the benefits of your location-independent lifestyle. Embrace the opportunity to make a positive difference, and create a more fulfilling and responsible digital nomad experience.

OVERCOMING CHALLENGES AND EMBRACING GROWTH

Dealing with setbacks and unexpected situations

As a digital nomad, you'll inevitably encounter challenges and unexpected situations that can test your resilience and adaptability. In this chapter, we'll discuss strategies for overcoming setbacks and embracing personal growth during your location-independent journey.

1. Cultivate a growth mindset: Embrace challenges as opportunities for growth and learning. Adopt a positive attitude and view setbacks as valuable experiences that can help you become more resourceful, adaptable, and resilient.

2. Develop problem-solving skills: Strengthen your problem-solving abilities by actively seeking solutions when faced with challenges. Break down problems into smaller components, brainstorm possible solutions, and evaluate their effectiveness.

3. Build a support network: Establish connections with fellow digital nomads, locals, and friends back home who can provide emotional support, advice, and practical assistance during difficult times.

4. Practice self-compassion: Be kind to yourself when setbacks occur, recognizing that everyone encounters challenges and that setbacks are a natural part of the digital nomad experience. Give yourself the same understanding and compassion you would offer a friend in a similar situation.

5. Manage stress effectively: Develop healthy coping mechanisms for managing stress, such as engaging in regular exercise, practicing mindfulness, and seeking social support.

6. Plan for the unexpected: Prepare for unforeseen challenges by maintaining a contingency fund, having backup plans, and being knowledgeable about local resources and services.

7. Be flexible and adaptable: Embrace change and uncertainty as integral aspects of the digital nomad lifestyle. Cultivate a sense of flexibility and adaptability that enables you to respond effectively to new situations and environments.

8. Seek feedback and learn from experiences: Regularly assess your progress, seek feedback from others, and reflect on your experiences. Use this information to inform your future decisions and develop strategies for overcoming similar challenges in the future.

9. Embrace lifelong learning: Continuously seek opportunities to learn and grow, both personally and professionally. Invest in your personal development by attending workshops, enrolling in courses, or engaging in self-study.

10. Celebrate your achievements: Acknowledge and celebrate your accomplishments, both big and small. Recognizing your successes can boost your self-confidence, motivation, and resilience during challenging times.

By embracing growth and learning to effectively navigate setbacks and unexpected situations, you can enhance your resilience, adaptability, and overall success as a digital nomad. Use these experiences as opportunities to strengthen your skills, expand your horizons, and deepen your understanding of yourself and the world around you.

Cultivating resilience and adaptability

Resilience and adaptability are essential traits for digital nomads, as they enable you to navigate challenges, embrace change, and thrive in the constantly evolving landscape of location-independent living. In this chapter, we'll discuss strategies for cultivating resilience and adaptability in your digital nomad journey.

1. Embrace a growth mindset: Approach challenges as opportunities to learn and grow. Develop a positive attitude toward setbacks and view them as valuable experiences that help you become more resourceful and adaptable.

2. Foster self-awareness: Reflect on your strengths, weaknesses, values, and priorities. Understanding yourself better will help you make informed decisions, adapt to new environments, and cope with challenges more effectively.

3. Develop problem-solving skills: Strengthen your ability to analyse problems, generate solutions, and evaluate their effectiveness. This skill set will be invaluable in overcoming obstacles and adapting to unexpected changes.

4. Be open to change: Recognize that change is an inherent part of the digital nomad lifestyle. Embrace uncertainty and be willing to let go of preconceived notions and plans in order to adapt to new situations.

5. Cultivate a strong support network: Build connections with fellow digital nomads, locals, and friends back home who can provide guidance, encouragement, and assistance when you face challenges.

6. Learn from failure: Instead of dwelling on mistakes, analyse the situation to identify lessons and opportunities for growth. Use these insights to make better decisions and improve your resilience in the future.

7. Set realistic expectations: Establish achievable goals and be prepared for the possibility of setbacks. Being realistic about your expectations will help you adapt more easily to changes and maintain a positive outlook.

8. Practice self-care: Prioritize your physical, emotional, and mental well-being by establishing routines and engaging in activities that promote relaxation, stress relief, and overall health. A strong foundation of self-care will enhance your resilience and adaptability.

9. Seek out new experiences: Actively pursue new experiences, opportunities, and challenges that push you outside of your comfort zone. This will help you build confidence in your ability to adapt and grow.

10. Reflect on and celebrate your achievements: Regularly assess your progress, recognize your successes, and celebrate your accomplishments. This will not only boost your self-confidence but also reinforce your resilience and adaptability in the face of challenges.

By cultivating resilience and adaptability, you'll be better equipped to navigate the uncertainties and challenges that come with the digital nomad lifestyle. Embrace these traits as essential components of your location-independent journey, and use them to thrive in the ever-changing world of remote work and travel.

Embracing personal growth and continuous learning

Personal growth and continuous learning are essential for thriving as a digital nomad, as they enable you to expand your skill set, adapt to new challenges, and enhance your overall well-being. In this chapter, we'll discuss strategies for embracing personal growth and continuous learning in your location-independent journey.

1. Set personal and professional goals: Establish clear, achievable goals that align with your values and aspirations. Regularly assess your progress, and adjust your goals as necessary to ensure continued growth and development.

2. Adopt a growth mindset: Embrace challenges as opportunities for learning and personal growth. Maintain a positive attitude toward setbacks and view them as valuable experiences that help you become more resourceful and adaptable.

3. Engage in lifelong learning: Continuously seek opportunities to expand your knowledge and skills, both personally and professionally. Attend workshops, enrol in courses, or engage in self-directed learning to stay current in your field and grow as an individual.

4. Develop self-awareness: Reflect on your strengths, weaknesses, values, and priorities. Understanding yourself better will help you make informed decisions, set meaningful goals, and pursue personal growth more effectively.

5. Cultivate resilience and adaptability: Embrace change and uncertainty as integral aspects of the digital nomad lifestyle. Build your resilience and adaptability by actively engaging with challenges and learning from your experiences.

6. Seek feedback and mentorship: Actively seek feedback from peers, colleagues, and mentors to identify areas for improvement and growth. Engage in open and honest conversations to gain new insights and perspectives.

7. Build a strong support network: Establish connections with fellow digital nomads, locals, and friends back home who can provide guidance, encouragement, and support as you pursue personal growth and continuous learning.

8. Practice self-compassion: Be kind to yourself when setbacks occur, recognizing that everyone encounters challenges and that setbacks are a natural part of personal growth. Give yourself the understanding and compassion you would offer a friend in a similar situation.

9. Embrace new experiences: Actively pursue new experiences, opportunities, and challenges that push you outside of your comfort zone. This will help you build confidence in your ability to adapt, learn, and grow.

10. Reflect on and celebrate your achievements: Regularly assess your progress, recognize your successes, and celebrate your accomplishments. Acknowledging your growth and achievements can boost your motivation, self-confidence, and commitment to continuous learning.

By embracing personal growth and continuous learning, you'll be better equipped to navigate the uncertainties and challenges that come with the digital nomad lifestyle. Use these strategies to foster a lifelong commitment to self-improvement, and create a more fulfilling and successful location-independent experience.

CONCLUSION

The ongoing journey of digital nomad mastery

As you reach the end of this book, it's important to recognize that the pursuit of digital nomad mastery is an ongoing journey, not a destination. As you continue to embrace the location-independent lifestyle, you'll encounter new challenges, opportunities, and experiences that will shape your growth, both personally and professionally.

1. Embrace the journey: Recognize that digital nomad mastery is a continuous process of learning, adapting, and evolving. Approach your location-independent journey with curiosity, openness, and a commitment to lifelong growth.

2. Reflect on your progress: Regularly assess your progress, celebrate your successes, and acknowledge the lessons learned from your setbacks. Use these insights to inform your future decisions and to refine your approach to the digital nomad lifestyle.

3. Stay adaptable and resilient: Embrace change and uncertainty as integral aspects of the digital nomad experience. Cultivate resilience and adaptability, which will serve you well as you navigate the ever-changing landscape of remote work and travel.

4. Prioritize personal growth and continuous learning: Actively pursue opportunities for personal and professional development. Embrace lifelong learning as a cornerstone of digital nomad mastery and seek out experiences that challenge and enrich you.

5. Foster meaningful connections: Build and maintain relationships with fellow digital nomads, locals, and friends back home. Nurture a strong support network that can provide guidance, encouragement, and camaraderie on your journey.

6. Give back and make a positive impact: Actively seek ways to contribute to the communities you visit and to support sustainable practices. Embrace the opportunity to make a difference and to foster a more responsible and fulfilling digital nomad experience.

7. Remain open to new experiences: Stay curious and open-minded, embracing new opportunities and challenges that arise during your travels. These experiences will contribute to your growth and deepen your understanding of yourself and the world around you.

8. Maintain balance and well-being: Prioritize your physical, emotional, and mental well-being by establishing routines, self-care practices, and a healthy work-life balance. A sustainable digital nomad lifestyle requires a strong foundation of self-care and well-being.

9. Share your knowledge and experiences: Connect with fellow digital nomads and travellers, sharing your insights, lessons learned, and experiences. By doing so, you can support and inspire others on their own journeys toward digital nomad mastery.

10. Enjoy the journey: Embrace the excitement, freedom, and adventure that come with the digital nomad lifestyle. Celebrate your accomplishments, cherish your experiences, and savour the memories you create along the way.

As you continue your journey toward digital nomad mastery, remember that the path is filled with countless opportunities for growth, exploration, and adventure. Embrace each moment, stay curious and open-hearted, and let your experiences guide you toward a more fulfilling and successful location-independent life.

Building a fulfilling and successful location-independent lifestyle

Creating a fulfilling and successful location-independent lifestyle requires a balance of personal and professional growth, adaptability, and a commitment to living intentionally. In this chapter, we'll explore strategies to help you build a thriving digital nomad experience.

1. Set clear goals and intentions: Establish personal and professional goals that align with your values and aspirations. Regularly assess your progress and adjust your goals as needed to ensure continued growth and satisfaction.

2. Cultivate a growth mindset: Embrace challenges as opportunities for learning and personal growth. Maintain a positive attitude toward setbacks and view them as valuable experiences that help you become more resourceful and adaptable.

3. Prioritize personal growth and continuous learning: Pursue opportunities for personal and professional development. Engage in lifelong learning to stay current in your field and grow as an individual.

4. Build a strong support network: Establish connections with fellow digital nomads, locals, and friends back home who can provide guidance, encouragement, and support as you navigate the location-independent lifestyle.

5. Develop resilience and adaptability: Embrace change and uncertainty as integral aspects of the digital nomad experience. Strengthen your resilience and adaptability to better navigate the ever-changing landscape of remote work and travel.

6. Focus on work-life balance: Establish routines and boundaries that promote a healthy balance between work, leisure, and self-care. Regularly evaluate your work-life balance and make adjustments as needed to maintain a sustainable and fulfilling lifestyle.

7. Engage with local communities: Immerse yourself in the cultures and communities you visit. Build relationships with locals, participate in cultural activities, and support local businesses to create meaningful connections and enrich your travel experiences.

8. Practice mindfulness and gratitude: Cultivate a practice of mindfulness and gratitude to help you stay present, appreciate the journey, and maintain a positive outlook on your experiences.

9. Prioritize health and well-being: Develop routines and self-care practices that support your physical, emotional, and mental health. Staying healthy and grounded is essential for maintaining a fulfilling location-independent lifestyle.

10. Give back and make a positive impact: Seek ways to contribute to the communities you visit, support sustainable practices, and make a positive impact on the world as you travel.

By incorporating these strategies, you can create a fulfilling and successful location-independent lifestyle that aligns with your values, fosters personal and professional growth, and enriches your travel experiences. Embrace the journey with curiosity and intention, and let your experiences guide you toward a thriving digital nomad life.

We know you appreciate how valuable reviews are to both the creators and the potential buyers of a book. Reviews help authors to improve their writing and encourage them to continue creating content that readers enjoy. They also help other readers to make informed decisions about whether a book is right for them.

www.ingramcontent.com/pod-product-compliance
Lightning Source LLC
Chambersburg PA
CBHW070336240526
45466CB00027B/2100